I0101475

FUNBARRASSING 2

Other books by
Shawn L. McMaster

FUNBARRASSING:
50
Funny and Embarrassing
Moments That Will
Probably Happen
to You!

FUNBARRASSING 2:
50
Moments That Will Probably NOT Happen to You!

Shawn L. McMaster

Copyright © 2023 Shawn L. McMaster

All rights reserved.

ISBN:979-8-218-30062-3

This book is dedicated to my family,
my friends, and all the crazy
things that will probably
NOT happen to us!

#1
You will probably
NOT see a
Big Foot!

#2
You will probably NOT be eaten by a shark!

#3
You will probably NOT be class valedictorian!

#4
You will probably NOT win the lottery!

#5
You will probably NOT get abducted by an alien!

#6
You will probably NOT have dinner with the president!

#7
You will probably NOT save the world!

#8
You will probably NOT meet your great great great grandparents!

#9
You will probably NOT be in a movie!

#10
You will probably NOT become a famous singer!

#11
You will probably
NOT drive a
Monster
Truck!

#12
You will probably NOT fly an airplane!

#13
You will probably
NOT find gold
in the hills!

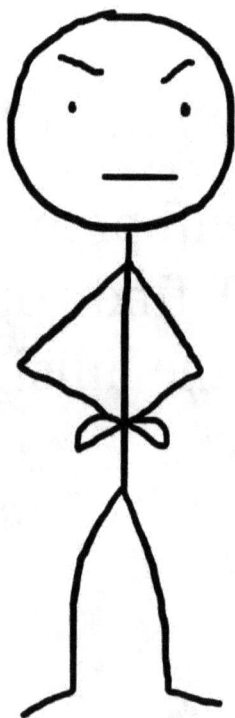

#14
You will probably NOT find out who stole your bike!

#15
You will probably NOT find the end of a rainbow!

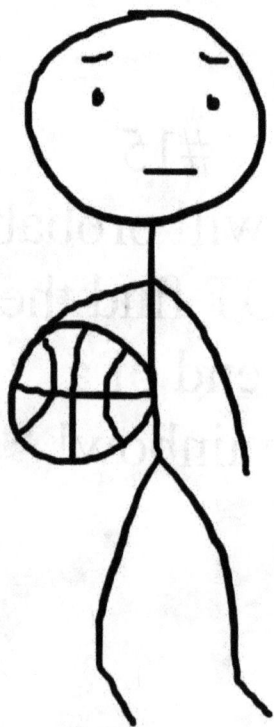

#16
You will probably NOT play on a professional sports team!

#17
You will probably
NOT drag race
the quarter mile
in under ten
seconds!

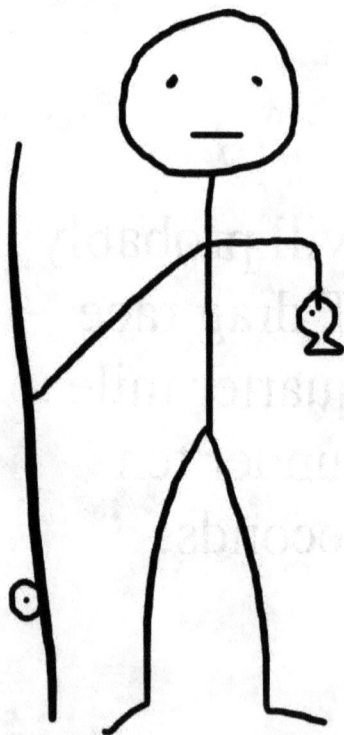

#18
You will probably NOT catch a world record fish!

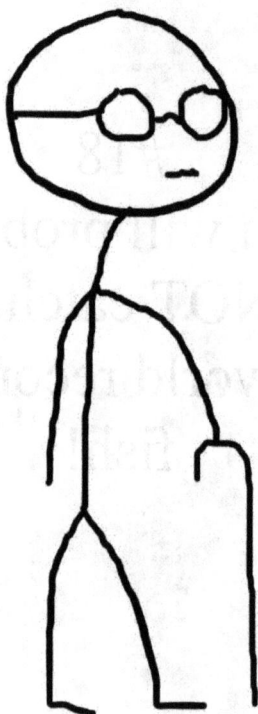

#19
You will probably
NOT live
forever!

#20
You will probably NOT be in the Olympics!

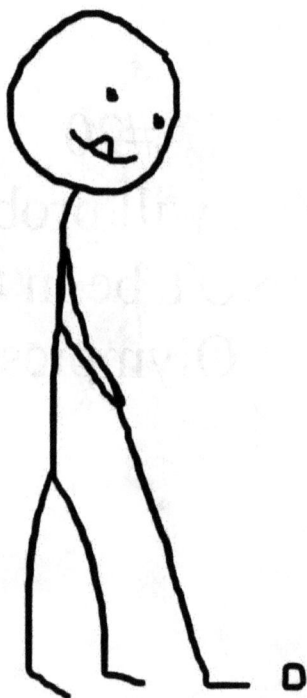

#21
You will probably NOT make a hole in one while out golfing!

#22
You will probably NOT go in the ocean and in the snow on the same day!

#23
You will probably NOT find a bunch of money!

#24
You will probably NOT go to outer space!

#25
You will probably NOT surf a wave that is taller than twenty feet!

#26
You will probably NOT ride a wheelie on your bike!

#27
You will probably NOT drop in on a big halfpipe!

#28
You will probably
NOT sail around
the world!

#29
You will probably
NOT find a
sunken
ship!

#30
You will probably
NOT go to
prison!

#31
You will probably NOT make money in the stock market!

#32
You will probably NOT get your money back from someone!

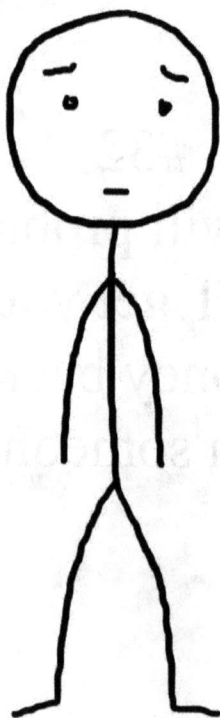

#33
You will probably
NOT win a
spelling
bee!

#34
You will probably NOT get a good deal from an auto dealer!

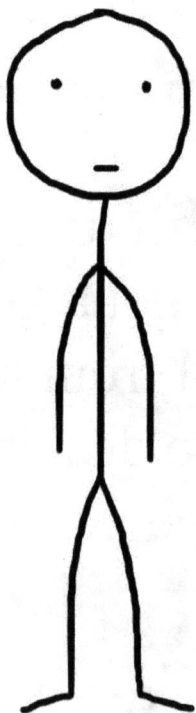

#35
You will probably NOT be a millionaire!

#36
You will probably NOT poke your eye out with a bb gun!

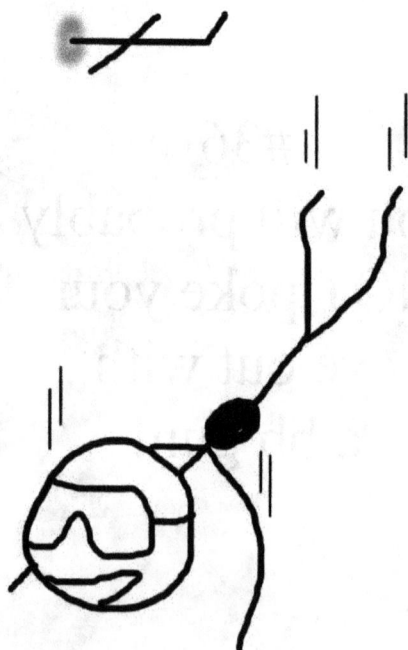

#37
You will probably
NOT go skydiving!

#38
You will probably NOT get the sticker you wanted from the vending machine!

#39
You will probably
NOT play a tape
or cd again!

#40
You will probably
NOT appear on
a talk show!

#41
You will probably NOT win a Nobel Prize!

#42
You will probably NOT stay young forever!

#43
You will probably NOT become a famous painter!

#44
You will probably NOT write a famous book!

#45
You will probably NOT fly in a helicopter!

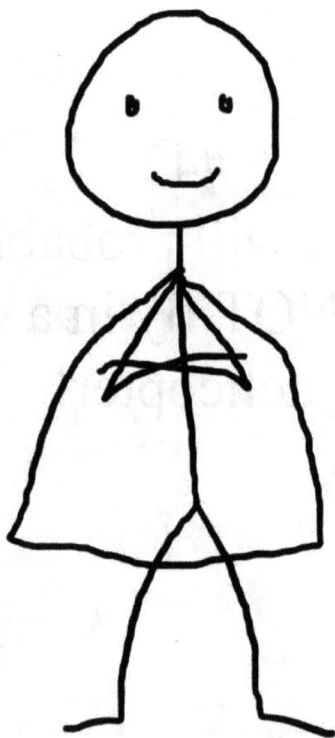

#46
You will probably
NOT become
a superhero!

#47
You will probably NOT be fluent in three or more languages!

#48
You will probably NOT get hurt by a ghost, so quit being afraid!

#49
You will probably NOT streak in public!

#50
You will probably NOT drive your car over 100 mph!

Shawn L. McMaster
is the author of the Funbarrassing
book series. He is from and lives
in California.

www.ingramcontent.com/pod-product-compliance
Lightning Source LLC
Chambersburg PA
CBHW071338290326
41933CB00039B/1649